SUCCESS IS FREE

...Only if you are ready to pay the price

Adeeko Olalekan

ISBN: 978-978-988-601-2

Cover design: Allen Zitto

Editing: Oluwatobi Adesanya

Published by:
Heart2World Publishing
info@heart2worldpublishing.org
30, Muyiwa Opaleye street. Surulere

For information on distribution, translation, or bulk sales,
please contact
Adeeko Olalekan
Phone: +2348104662053
Email: Olalekan.adeeko@yahoo.com

Dedication

I dedicate this book to the Almighty God the giver of life, strength, wisdom, and understanding.

CONTENT

INTRODUCTION

Before you dive into this book, I want you to look inwards; take a close look at your present situation and ask yourself- "Am I where I want to be?"

Do you desire a better life, to be more, and to accomplish more? Certainly you do. I wrote this book to serve as a driving force to help you scale the walls of your doubts and fears on to the other side where your dreams and aspirations lie.

As you read each chapter of this book and put to practice the principles therein, your success will be guaranteed.

CHAPTER 

SELF-DETERMINATION

SELF DETERMINATION

"I am not what happened to me, I am what I choose to become."
- Carl Gustav Jung

I've always been curious about the keys to success, and in all my search, one thing stood out for me; no one ever accomplished anything great without determination.

As simple as the word "determination" is, it should be treated with a high level of respect. Show me great men who accomplished great things without determination and I'll dig into their story, take you back to a point in their lives when they were determined and optimistic to do great things. In order to change who you are and your present situation, you need to be determined. Determination is the booster. Though I started this book with the concept of self-determination, every other chapter of this book ties together as one whole. It doesn't matter your background, your race, or colour, the principles here will guide you to greatness.

I believe that life is what you think and make of it. Here in Africa, it is often believed that when life isn't going as smoothly as desired, it is because there are certain mystical forces at work or a wicked personality in the cover of darkness conjuring some voodoo to prevent one from succeeding. I laugh out loud whenever I hear these narratives. It's even more nauseating knowing that these narratives are pushed, not only by young people, but adults as well. You find them saying such absurd and obnoxious things, and this they pass on to the young ones. If you are a youth and you still do not have a mind of your own, you are likely to also share in those beliefs, live it out, and teach others to do same.

You have to possess a mind of your own. You have to change the state of your mind, change your beliefs, see all things as possible, be positive-minded, goal-oriented, purpose-driven and determined. This is not to imply that you won't encounter challenges. I encountered challenges and I'm still encountering challenges—big ones at that; but with the right state of mind, coupled with the determination to succeed, the sky is just the starting point.

There's nothing impossible under the sun. I put it to you that you are the only person mitigating your advancement in life and destiny. Just as there is a thin line between life and death, there is also a thin line between success and failure. You might want to say that I don't understand or know how much you have failed, but I tell you, you don't know and can't quantify the number of failures I have encountered right from my high school days, through my college days till now. I'll tell you about one of the events of the past that left an indelible mark in my life:

I gained admission into a college in Nigeria in the year 2012 where I started my first two-year diploma journey. While in school, I encountered some challenges financially, emotionally and all you could think of. Still, I pressed on, wrote all my exams even when I had to skip classes sometimes to do some menial jobs to sustain myself. I have always being a self-reliant person. But in this season of my life, I really had to take charge of my own fate. The financial situation in my family bore no hope for me, so I had to fend for myself all through.

Just as I was rounding off and about to write my final exams, my mom was diagnosed with Breast Cancer. This weighed me down emotionally and mentally, but I pressed on with my studies and finished my exams after which I left for home immediately. My mom later passed on Christmas day, 2017. I faced my life squarely, started tutoring students and doing all sort of jobs I could lay my hands on. During this period, I totally forgot about my school and certificate. I didn't even check my portal for my final year results, all I said to myself was I know I'm not that poor academically and whenever I need my results and certificate, I'll request for them, no matter how many years may have passed by.

Some years later, I applied to a university in the United States despite getting my visa denied over and over again. I was at the verge of uploading my credentials when I suddenly got the urge to go get my results. I arrived at the Admissions Office and I was informed that my result was no longer on the school portal, years had passed but I could still find it if I went to my Head of Department's office to go check by myself. I got there and to my surprise, I saw my result with a reference! YES! You read that right! - A reference, and there was no way I could take the paper or course again. The suggested solution was to enrol and start all over. I turned around with my heavy legs and left his office on that fateful day. The rest is history and that's just a tip of my self-inflicted failures, so it doesn't matter how difficult your situation is- with the right mindset, filled with determination, success is guaranteed.

Challenges and tribulations are inevitable. Even Jesus said, *"In this world you shall have tribulations but be of good cheer, I have overcome the world."* Your attitude and disposition during the time of challenges will determine how far you will go in life. It will determine if you are fit to walk into your greatness and see your heart desires fulfilled.

Also remember this saying, "If wishes were horses, beggars would ride", it's not enough to wish and desire great things. this quote reveals that having good intentions or wishes won't make you great.

Self-determination comes from within, it is a resolve to be and to do the needful as it relates to your goals and desire for accomplishment. This implies that self-determination can't be enforced, it can't be impacted or transferred from one person to the other. It is, rather, a free personal compulsion. This also implies that if you don't take steps to move from where you are, you'd remain on the same spot till you decide to take the bold step.

As powerful as the law of attraction is, if you don't make up your mind, it will be impossible or difficult for the law of attraction to work for you. If there is no clear understanding and determination of what you want from life, the law of attraction will remain helpless as there's nothing to work on. The law of attraction attracts to you whatsoever it is you want or desire to have from the bottom of your heart. This powerful law can attract anything you want to yourself. You'll eventually get what you desire as long as you keep the picture in your heart and you press forward (despite all odds) with determination to succeed.

Quickly, I will share with you the three principles of self-determination.

Freedom:

This is simply the ability to determine how you want to live your life. As mentioned earlier, you are the architect of your life, whatsoever you do today will either make you or mar you in the future.

The freedom you create today should and must be used judiciously. Ever since I was a kid, thanks to my parents, I have experienced freedom when it comes to making decisions. I have been able to have a mind of my own which has grown stronger and stronger, day after day. Freedom shouldn't be taken with levity, but rather with proper actions and choices. The choice you make will be the one to position you either for greatness or not, choice is very powerful as it can also make you or mar you, the power of choices should not be taken for granted, as choices are powerful elements of self-determination.

For you to be self-determined, you would have weighed your chances and arrived at your very own choice of conditions. This will be a propelling factor to keep you going in the direction of achieving your dreams, goals and aspirations. Life, I tell you, is so flexible and malleable; you have the power to make of it whatsoever you want or wish, provided you have got the key ingredients needed to make things happen. You can come from a wretched family and become the wealthiest man.

Life, I tell you, gives to you whatever you request of it, just as I have mentioned earlier, there is a thin line between success and failure and this, you shouldn't forget at all, no matter what, or where you are, you are the only reactant that can start up your reaction, with adequate combination with the right catalysts (keys), the result of greatness and success is ascertained. We all love good things, and you would agree with me they don't come on a platter of gold, you have to know the smart and right moves to take in order to receive them. With the right mind and a clear vision, you can become the next wealthiest man the next day. As little as the mind might seem to be, it has got the power to take you places that you have never dreamt of before.

With the right state of mind, filled with great ideas and goals, the likelihood of achieving success is 70 percent, and of course, you would agree with me that that is a good grade to start with. There is no doubt at all about the power of the mind. The mind of the human creature travels even faster than the speed of light itself; take for instance, you can be on your couch and there you are plugging your mind to envisage where you want to be thirty years from now, right from where you are. Wow!!! Isn't that amazing and great? We are complete beings, I say to you, you are a special being, take a look at yourself now and say with a smile to yourself these words, "I am special and rare!" How do you feel after doing this, I know you feel great! Do you know we just built up our self-esteems?

I say to you, you can't become great, successful or move from where you are to the point where you want to be without first uplifting your esteem, feeling good about who you are and being grateful for where you are presently, you've got all the freedom you need. Freedom is a powerful tool which we all possess but fail to use appropriately. Sometimes, I see people misuse freedom and I can't but wonder why they do so. Being thankful allows you to see the goodness of where you are presently. The right act of gratitude over little things will open doors to more things to be grateful for. In other words, be grateful for everything you enjoy or that which makes you happy now however little they may be or seem, I say to you, there's more about life to be enjoyed and experienced. You know, while growing, all I could ever think of was that I want to be great and leave the earth making a positive impact; all I ever wanted was my name, Olalekan Adeeko, to be known for great things, leaving remarkable and happy moments in the lives of whosoever came across me or my book. The journey of self-determination started right from my college days,. All I wanted to do was to make it, be great and famous, leaving remarkable footprints in the hearts and minds of men. I started working towards it, doing everything that will push me further towards achieving my dream,. I failed over and over, still failing, but I didn't stop working, growing and learning from my mistakes.

At first, I thought failure was a bad thing. As time went on, I realized that failure is actually part of the equation of success. For me, this meant that giving up after failing should never be an option.

I never knew I would write a book, never have I thought about that. But along the road to becoming great and making impact, I found myself doing this. To accomplish my goal of writing a book, I had to acquire knowledge. I read new books, studied new techniques about writing and anything I could lay my hands on. Left to some people, they would have given up and said, "Hey! I don't think this writing thing is for me, maybe I was just joking around." I knew I had the freedom to make my choices and the choice I make at that moment will either make or mar my dream and goals. With self-determination, I let loose and started anyhow and any way. I knew I would engage the right hands much later to review and vet the book before it eventually gets published.

Most people will think "He's a good writer and he's been writing for a long time!" or "Oh wow! He's must have written other books before now." That's not true. This is my first book! How do you feel after reading that? I say to you, freedom is part of the principle of self-determination.

Responsibility:

This is also a key principle to self determination. I would say to you without the act of being responsible in all areas of life, the journey of self-determination leading to success may not be fulfilled.

With freedom being the first principle of self-determination, responsibility also plays a major role. To be responsible is a tall order. Many will rather blame others or pass the buck around. A lot of people want to enjoy benefits, but they do not want to be responsible for making it happen.

Being responsible is key. Now, if you want to change how to see your problems, you have to change what you value and how you measure failure and success.

Here's something I want to share with you from what I read on a blog some time ago.

We're often told to take 100% responsibility for our lives. What is the big deal about it? The big deal is that it moves you from being a victim to victor.

It puts you at cause and not at effect, meaning that you accept that you create your life and you're not just reacting to it. You appreciate that things happen for you and not to you.

Taking responsibility puts you at choice and that allows you to choose how to respond to life's challenges. You move into the driver seat of your life's journey.

Most of all, taking 100% responsibility changes your energy and the practices described here put you in higher vibrating mind-body states.

As you know, we are energy; our thoughts, feelings, words and actions are energy and the law of attraction brings us more of what we think and feel. It matches the energy of your thoughts and feelings with experiences that will give you the same energy.

Now, when you broadcast thoughts that result in you feeling good, the law of attraction responds by bringing you the experiences that will confirm you feeling good.

So, it pays to take responsibility of your life. Do you agree?

Let's explore 9 ways how this looks in everyday life, including your business.

1. Take responsibility for your thoughts, feelings, words and actions

To take responsibility for your life, is to take responsibility for your powers of thinking, feeling, speaking and acting, because this is the structure of all human experience. You create your life with your thoughts, feelings, words and actions.

You take responsibility when you accept that the thoughts you have are thoughts coming from your mind. How you feel happens in your body and is as a result of your thoughts. The words you speak come from your mouth and voice. The actions you take are taken by you.

What this means is that nobody can make you think, feel, say or do anything. Nobody can push your buttons, because you are the button maker! In the same way you don't have control over how other people respond, as they respond from their mindset.

2. Stop blaming

Stop blaming your partner, parents, economy, your upbringing or the dog for your misfortune. Blaming keeps you in victim mode and robs you of changing your situation.

When you stop blaming and start accepting responsibility, you shift from victim to victor. Now, you can look at the situation and decide what to do about it.

Ask yourself, "What is my role in this?"

3. Stop complaining

Complaining is another form of blaming and playing victim as if you have no choice. It also shows that you focus on lack, things going wrong, things happening to you. In everything not going according to plan, there is a gift, there is a bigger picture.

Ask yourself, "What is the gift here? What can I learn from this?"

4. Refuse to take anything personally

This is a big deal! If you take any form of disagreement as a personal attack, remember you don't have control over how other people respond, you only have control over how you respond.

Refuse to take anything personally. It is most probably not about you, but about the issue at hand. Instead of making assumptions, ask questions. This is a very powerful and liberating practice, with never ending surprises.

Ask yourself, "Is this about me or the issue at hand?"

5. Make yourself happy

Taking responsibility for your happiness is liberating. First, you have to realise that happiness does not come from outside of you. It is not the job of your partner, parent, friend, child, to make you happy.

To be happy is a decision and the gateway to happiness is gratitude. Keep a gratitude journal and you will find a lot to be happy about.

Also, do things that make you feel happy. Listen to your favourite music, surround yourself with beauty, express your creativity, do acts of kindness, etc.

Ask yourself, "What about this could make me happy?"

6. Live in the present moment

Life is now. There is only one moment, Now. The past is history, the future is a mystery, so there is only now; this moment. Take responsibility for this moment and make the best of it to redeem the past and create the future you want. Paulo Coelho wrote something to this effect in his biography.

Be the gatekeeper of your thoughts and refuse to have a rerun of the same 60,000 thoughts of yesterday if they do not get you what you want in life.

Choose your thoughts carefully in every moment and when you become present you have the awareness of what you are thinking and feeling. This then allows you to interrupt thoughts that do not serve you. Deliberately change them in the moment to what you want to create in that moment to shape your future.

Ask yourself, "Am I in the present moment and what do I want?"

7. Use the power of intention

You have the power to choose. In fact, you make choices all the time. Tea or coffee, red dress or black dress, hair up or down, yoga or go for a run. Even by not making a choice, you are making a choice.

Become intentional about making choices by having a vision in mind. A vision for your life, your business, your relationship, your health, wealth, etc.

Living intentionally by deliberately making choices to move you towards manifesting your vision or outcomes is consciously taking responsibility for your life.

Ask, "Is saying yes to this moving me towards my goal?"

8. Feel calm and confident

When you take responsibility for your life and experience, you step into a place of calm confidence. You feel calm because you know that you are consciously in charge of yourself and that you can choose how you respond.

You feel confident that you will not fall into victim-mode by sucking up other people's verbal vomit. They can keep those gifts.

Ask yourself, "What do I choose to accept from this conversation and how do I choose to respond?"

9. Look for the good in people

There's a saying that we judge ourselves by our intentions and we judge others by their behaviour.

Make it your new habit to look for the intentions behind people's behaviours. So often, when we understand where someone comes from, we let go of judgment.

One excellent practice is to remove the labels we hang on to people like bibs around their necks and that somehow give us permission to treat them in the worst possible way. This often applies to the people closest to us.

Ask yourself, "If I just see him/her as a human being, how will I respond differently?"

Another effective practice is listening to understand instead of listening to respond. This means to practice asking questions to really understand what the other person means, instead of waiting for a chance to interrupt and voice your important opinion.

This allows you to take responsibility to intentionally have illuminating conversations and fulfilling relationships, because the person that you are talking to will appreciate your attention, and, in return, trust and support you.

To conclude this session of responsibility I'll tell you this, to achieve great success, you and only you should take responsibility for your actions.

Support:

Support as a principle of self-determination simply means organising resources in ways that are life changing and meaningful. Let's break it down- when we talk about resources, the first thing you have to consider or prerequisite you have to possess in order to be able to use support is that you have to be sure of what and where you want to be in life. In other words, you have to possess a clear picture of your goals, no matter how daunting they may appear.

Knowing this will help you know what steps to take in achieving them and also the kind of support required. Take for instance, I want to be a successful public speaker, that's my goal, now how do I become a successful public speaker?

- I have to watch the clips of great speakers both past and present, continuously.
- I have to take courses that pertain to public speaking.
- I have to attend seminars and conferences.
- I have to watch TED shows.
- I have to read books on public speaking.
- I have to indulge in continuous practice and fluency in my spoken words.

Now, let's talk about the resources; don't forget the resources must align with our current life changing process. Resources that will be needed to be a successful speaker are, books to read on public speaking, adequate maximisation of time, money etc.

As you know, being self-determined means making things happen in your life. With these above listed resources, you will agree with me that the journey to becoming a successful public speaker is 60- 80 percent covered. With this knowledge, you can and will be confident to address any gathering however small or large.

Doing this constantly will secure a platform to help you build up your career to its peak. You are not created to be unsuccessful. You are the greatest creature that has ever lived, there is no replica of you, you have got the power to be great in you. All you need is to be determined and align yourself with your goals, getting yourself the support needed to becoming successful.

Yes, you need support to be successful, both internal and external. The more valid a dream is, the more support it requires.

An illustration is like a building, a building can't stand alone unless it is supported by a foundation, columns, beams or pillars. A life without any internal or external support towards success is bound to fall by the way side.

Never take the power of support for granted; if you want to move far in life you need support. Another thing I want you to realise is that, successful people are confident and can lead themselves, as well as others. They have their own vision and mission and seek to bring it to life on a daily basis. They also know who they aren't and don't waste time on things that they aren't good at or satisfied with.

Some years back, there was an interview conducted, to hear different individuals share their opinions about success, and these were the responses.

"Success is defined by who we are, what we believe in, and what we think it means to be successful. For some, it is money; for others, it could be relationships, family, jobs, religion, or education. I believe that success is reaching my own personal dreams. I'm not done with my dreams, but know that I have been successful so far because I've worked toward my goals regardless of my disability." –College student who is deaf.

"Success is possessing the capability for self-determination. Self-determination is the ability to decide what I want to do with my life, and then to act on that decision.

"A successful life is one where I can be actively engaged in creative activities that make a contribution to the lives of others. Success is a kind of by-product and NOT an end in itself!" –Professor who is blind

"To me, having a successful life is being able to do things independently for myself, and not always have someone there to do things for me. It's achieving my goals on my own terms and at my own pace."–High school student.

The three principles mentioned and explained above show carefully that there are basic things we have to do. In other words, there are basic actions we have to take in order to attain our peak. With determination, coupled with freedom, responsibility and support, attaining success is guaranteed. You don't need to lay around, shying from the required things to do.

I'll say this to you, not everyone that wants success is ready to pay the price. There is a price to be paid to gain something tangible out of life. You have to pay a price to get your dream car; someone might ask, "What if I was given?" Well, the person who gave you has somehow paid the price before purchasing the car. As a student, to be successful in your studies, you have to study hard and work smart. This applies to all works of life. A successful entrepreneur pays the price of sleepless nights, research, connection, seeking funding and the likes.

It is known that God, the Almighty, didn't just bring the world into existence at once. The Bible says He worked for six days and on the seventh day he rested, meaning you have to be willing to push yourself, push yourself harder and harder!

While I was writing this book, it came with its own challenges. There were times I didn't feel like writing, times when I started writing and stopped. But the path to success is not as smooth as we think, we all have to go through some hurdles. There are times we won't feel like moving on with the journey, but I tell you, that is the time to press on, that is the time to make a refuel of your energy, have a new clear vision of what you want and where you want to be.

This I'll tell you - life wants you to be successful and also doesn't want you to be, so it depends on what you want to make of it. The two versions of life are constant and always looking for who will fall in; the question is which of the versions of life do you want to fall in?

If you want to be successful, are you ready to pay the price? Don't stand on the way hindering the advancement of others.

The journey to success comes with seasonal challenges, how you handle them determines your overall success in life.

CHAPTER 

SELF-DISCOVERY

> "I understood myself only after I destroyed myself.
> And only in the process of fixing myself, did I know who I really was."
>
> Sade Andria Zabala

This second key is vital and is also a prerequisite to being successful. Self-discovery is the process of learning more about yourself and who you are. Self-discovery helps to identify our abilities, but also how we can develop and leverage them.

Self-discovery should be a goal for everyone. Some people go through life playing a role to mask who they really are, others simply become what others want them to be, which won't allow room for great exploits. You will discover once you are doing what you really love to do and what truly gives you happiness, your impact becomes boundless.

Success comes from self-discovery. Take your time, look inwards, you own your mind, you know what you're capable of doing, you know what you can't do, you know your strengths, you know your weaknesses. There's always that one thing already deposited in you that will lead you to greatness. Sometimes, it might be more than one, but I tell you, everyone on the surface of the earth has one unique thing they can work on to be successful. All you need to do is look inwards, you need to discover yourself, don't do what others want you to do or become if that's not what you want. Never follow the multitude.

In the previous chapter, I shared on the price we have to pay to be successful, now, here is one price that requires no funds. Sit down, and think deep, discover yourself. I will tell you this; the process of self-discovery isn't what you do in a day. It surely starts one day, but it won't end in a day. You are bundle of treasure waiting to be unlocked. So, start today.

While trying to discover yourself, make sure you're not stagnant. Keep moving on your instincts, because during this process of discovery arise some instincts which must be acted upon, this will lead to your final destination which is being able to arrive at who you really are and what you can do to succeed. Remember I told you being successful is a state of mind, if you can't see it, you can't feel it, and can't have it.

Sometimes, you might be wondering and asking yourself

questions like; *Why hasn't anything changed for me? Why am I still on the same level after so long?* The answer is you haven't discovered the right channel for your discovery. You have to arrive at an appropriate, smart way of putting into action all your discoveries. This might, as well, lead to having the right information, knowledge, understanding and connection. If all these are achieved, you will find yourself on the path to being successful.

It's not enough to discover oneself, it also requires a lot of action; you have to be prepared to work hard and smart, you have to be consistent and diligent.

Failure should and must always be an avenue to foster your journey to success, this is to say that whenever you fail, you should and must always learn from it. I would tell you this, you can't always get it all right and going at once, you must be aware that it is a process. Just as it is not possible to build a mansion in a day, even so certain things in life require time to make them happen.

Never get tired or frustrated whenever things or circumstances don't go the way you planned. If all ideas and hard work were right and perfect, the world would only have few people striving to succeed.

Success is a thing of the mind, just like I stated earlier, "if you can't see it, you can't feel it, and can't have it". You have to be able to see- vision is highly important and essential, the possession of this will lead to the drive you need to achieve great success. Everything you see in life today was because someone conceived an idea, had a clear vision, and worked tirelessly to see it materialise.

Nothing exists without a purpose. You have a purpose here on earth too. Therefore, you must understand that it is not just enough to discover yourself, you need to take the right step with the right drive.

Quickly, I'd share this; after I discovered my passion for writing, among other things, can you believe that on many occasions I just didn't feel like writing? Many times, I would open up my laptop to write and the next minute, I shut down the laptop and then doze off. Now, let's take note, first, I was able to discover myself; leading to my passion, secondly, I was able to gather the resources and knowledge needed for me to be a writer or to write my very own book, and then, thirdly, I commenced writing. Remember that I said most times, I just didn't feel like writing, most times I closed my laptop whenever I was about to write. Now take a closer look to see what I was lacking, I lacked consistency, I lacked diligence and also discipline which would be discussed in the next chapter of this book. Note that I've got a drive, a goal, I have taken the right steps to knowing how to become a good writer, but having all these without the rest will just continue to make you go round the circle and at the end of the day, success might look unachievable. That is to remind us of the first observations and questions at the beginning of this paragraph.

This is to remind us of the popular saying, "When life gives you lemon, make lemonade", meaning you have to make do with what life gives you, however little you may think it is, no matter how stupid you might think your idea is, also note that the world won't buy a stupid idea, so your idea had better be valid. Where you are is not an excuse for failure or being unsuccessful; what you don't have presently is not an excuse for not exhibiting or getting out that idea, absence of resources doesn't mean you can't and won't be successful.

Success starts from you, in other words, it's inbuilt. If you can't see it, then you can't have it. You need to be determined, discover yourself and get ready to move to the next stage of your life.

You alone know your worth, and if you can't fight for it, it may be difficult to achieve that desired point or stage in life. I'll give us an example of a scenario that happened right in front of me; I have a friend who walked up to me one day and said, *"I have been asking myself if I actually live purposefully, I think I'm just being carried around like water waves"*.

When I heard this, I was so surprised and at the same time I wasn't because I'm glad he could get to a point where he could actually sit and reason within himself, that alone is a green light to success, because that will be a propelling factor to other things that must be done to be successful. His thoughts will lead to self-determination, then to self-discovery, and then it goes on like that,. You may be surprised to see the results in few months, why?

Being successful is a state of mind- until that mindset changes, nothing will change, you will just find out you keep on complaining, having big dreams and aspirations and yet on the same spot.

I need to say this: There are some doors failure opens. When failure comes knocking, all you need to do is to make sure it's pushing you to be a better version of yourself. In other words "fail forward" endeavour not to fail backwards.

Self-discovery is crucial to living an authentic life, be true to who you want to be by taking the journey within and discovering who you truly are.

I'll share with you some quotes I found about self-discovery which are related to the subject matter of this chapter:

- *"Knowing yourself is the beginning of wisdom" by Aristotle.*
- *"When I discover who I am I'll be free" by Ralph Ellison, Invisible Man.*
- *"We shall not cease from exploration And at the end of our exploring we'll be able to arrive at where we started And know the place for the first time." by T.S Eliot, Four Quartets.*
- *"Until you make the unconscious conscious, it will direct your life and you will call it faith" by C. G. Jung*

To go further, I'll introduce you to some self-discovery questions that will help you realise and arrive at who you really are and want to become. Some of these questions you already know and some you don't. I honestly want you to read and ponder on the questions over and over until you arrive at the best answer for yourself. It may take hours, days, or even months to provide detailed answers. In any case, attempt all of them before reading the next chapter of this book.

1- What's my purpose in life?
2- What is my personality type?
3- What are the three words that describe me best?
4- What matters to me most right now?
5- What scares me most right now?
6- Have I been holding myself back in any way?

7- What could I do to be happier?
8- What can I make happen that will lead to my success?
9- How am I living my life right now?
10- What are the factors mitigating my advancement?

I'm 90% sure that you will move to the next stage after carefully studying, and answering these life changing questions.

Remember, the sky is your starting point, and it's never too late to start now.

CHAPTER 

SELF-DISCIPLINE

SELF DISCIPLINE

"If I want to be great, I have to win
the victory over myself...self- discipline."

- Harry S. Truman

Oh well, I would like to welcome you to yet another germane chapter of this book. Without this key in your hands, a life of purpose and impact will be very difficult, if not impossible.

This key, I know, isn't new to many, but of course, it needs to be repeated. This key has been engaged by those who achieved great feats in different fields of endeavour and you can also engage it too.

To kick-start, I will like you to digest this quote I found very useful. It says, "With self-discipline" says Theodore Roosevelt, "almost anything is possible."

Yes! With self-discipline, almost anything is possible and I will also include achievable, so what else are you waiting for? The key to success is here again, all you need to do is get a hold of it and open your door to success. I know you will be successful, yes, I do, in case you think I'm referring to someone beside you NO! I'm referring to you reading this esteemed book from this unknown (now known) author, yes, you will be successful.

This is to encourage you not to give up on your journey to success. Nobody is born disciplined, you become disciplined. All successful people are disciplined. So, this is saying in order to be successful, you have to be disciplined, there is no short cut around it. If you are not ready to be disciplined, I'm sorry to say you are not ready for success.

Success and discipline go hand in hand, there is no way you can leave that aside, there is no way you can ignore that, it is a fundamental requirement on your journey to success.

I have grown to learn and master this act of self-discipline, and ever since I have seen significant changes in my own life. Things I procrastinated on, were no longer an issue for me to get done within a short time, and I find it easy whenever I carry them out. You must realize that you can become anything, you can unlearn an old habit and also learn new ones. You can learn to be disciplined as well.

It took me several years to understand, learn, and master the habit of self-discipline, but it was worth it.

This simply means that there is no stipulated time for you to learn and master the habit of self-discipline. In fact, if you learn it at an early stage, it is a great plus to you, also, if you start in your 30s or 40s, it's not too late. There is nothing you can't achieve at any particular point in time. NO TIME IS TOO LATE FOR YOUR DREAMS.

Self-discipline is a pattern of behaviour where you choose to do what you know you should do, whether or not you feel like it. It's the inner power that pushes you to get out of bed to exercise rather than sleep. It is the assertion of willpower over more basic desires. It is a habit, a practice, a philosophy and a way of life. To be more explicit, if I don't say this and I paint all as if it is very easy and smooth, then I am not being truthful to us- you and I. Self-discipline, like everything else, is a practice. Not every day will be perfect, but each day with its failures and small wins is progress, and to be frank that's basically what self-discipline is all about.

Here are some hints on how to build your self- discipline:

- Know where you struggle;
- Know how you succeed;

- Identify and write down clear goals;
- Visualise your outcome;
- Don't wait for it to feel right;
- Start small;
- Get a mentor;
- Practice, fail, start over.

Now, let's start by explaining each of these points accordingly:

- KNOW WHERE YOU STRUGGLE: To go about this, start by writing down what you do in a day. Then reflect on what you value and ask yourself whether your behaviour reflect those values. There are probably a few things you do each day that do not honour those values.

During the identification phase, it's helpful to ask for feedback from colleagues, mentors, and family members who know you best. See if there's an overlap between how others see your actions and how you've self-identified your weakness.

Once you've identified a few areas to improve, put together a plan of attack. For instance, if my weakness is in the area of procrastinating calling prospects until its too late in the day, the results will be glaring in my records. This literally puts me behind for the rest of the week and makes it tough to meet quota. To solve this problem, I could resolve that "Tomorrow, I'm going to make X number of calls immediately I arrive at the office in the morning."

- KNOW HOW YOU SUCCEED: You need to know what works for you, what you can do that will lead you to success, and the appropriate time for it to be done. You need to know what times you are productive; you shouldn't waste your time or trade it for anything.

You have to personally figure out the best time that works for you, i.e. when you must get things done and settled. You shouldn't postpone what you are meant to do at the time you know you are to do them. Take for example, if you are someone who is most active in the early hours of the day, you shouldn't fix or do anything that will take your mornings away from you. Your mornings are the best time to get things done. It is the right time to work on your goals, it is the right time to make that move, it is the right time to make that sacrifice. Do not postpone your important tasks till noon or evening for anything.

Everything you do on your way to success must be productive, if not all, the majority of things you do must be productive. Productivity is key. Do everything possible to set yourself up for success.

- IDENTIFY AND WRITE CLEAR GOALS: This is a must for everyone who wants to succeed. You can't overlook the aspect of writing down your goals, whether they are immediate, short-term, or long-term. While growing up, all I knew was to set my goals and write a long list of all my goals, they were not smart goals and for most of the things I wrote down, the responsibility wasn't on me to meet, my parents were responsible for their fulfilment. Now that I write this, I realize that that was a weak attempt at goal setting. There are three kinds of goals; immediate, short, and long term goals. Your immediate goals are the goals that must be met or achieved without delay. For instance, if your goal is to take your medicine three times daily, that's something that must be done without fail. Your health and well-being depends on it.

Your short-term goals are goals that must be achieved within a short stipulated time. An example is you securing a certain amount of money for your company in the span of two to four months. Then your long-term goals are goals that span for a long time, they are usually not immediate and, of course, not short-term. They could be between 10-20 years.

Success doesn't happen overnight, it happens over time. Success takes time. Except you've got a plan to go rob a bank, like the movie "Money Heist" you cannot become a millionaire overnight. I'm a big believer in miracles, but process is a huge part of success.

To add to all these, your goals have a greater tendency of being achieved when they are written down. The act of writing down your goals forces you to visualise the goal itself, how to achieve it, and what steps you need to take to get there. So, before you set out to become the best version of yourself —whether at work or in your personal life— identify your goals and write them down.

- VISUALISE YOUR OUTCOME: It is true that "If you can't see it, you can't feel it, and you can't have it." Let me state here: Your brain doesn't differentiate between what is real and what is imagined. So, when you imagine something vividly, your brain chemistry changes as if you actually experienced it. For most of us, we may have tried and ascertained that fact, and yes, if you're just starting, or you probably do not believe it, you can also try it out. You will be amazed at the result you'll get. All you need do is make visualisation a habit.

Goals visualised are accomplished faster than non-visualised ones. The law of attraction says it all, you can get what you want from life if you can see it. Life gives you anything you make or demand out of it, and also it draws you nearer to your visualised goals and aspirations, it appears or happens faster than you can think.

Visualising positive outcomes also brings positive feelings. For instance, you could write: "When I write and launch my next book, I'm going to treat myself to a classy dinner in a 5-star restaurant." Setting your goals this way will help you do away with fear while taking actionable steps towards the fulfilment of your goals. In the next chapter of this book, we will talk more about it.

- DON'T WAIT FOR IT TO FEEL RIGHT: Feelings are fickle. They are not reliable, you cannot depend on them to accomplish anything. Imagine if the sun depended on its feelings to fulfill their purpose, we'd have been dead long ago. You don't have till you "feel" its right before you set your goals and take the required actions. Just do it. Do not delay any longer, stop that procrastination; the more you wait the more you miss opportunities. There's no better than now to get started. Have you ever felt the pain of missing out on something just because you did not act early enough? I have, severally. And it is a painful experience. You really have to get ready before you feel ready.

Opportunities are everywhere, but they will not always be available. The car or house you saw at 30% off today will most likely not be available tomorrow. Take the needed steps now. It could be as simple as making a phone call, or walking into a place to make inquiries. These little action steps make a huge difference in the end. Don't delay.

Treasure every moment and squeeze out the opportunities locked within them.

- START SMALL: Do not despise small beginnings; if you want to advance in life, you must learn to start small. That is basically what growth is all about, you can't plant a seed and all of a sudden you expect it to become what you want it to be in the next couple of days. It takes a process, and of course, this process can't be skipped. It also requires a lot of patience; you have to be patient and always trust the process. On no occasion must you doubt yourself! I'm aware doubts might come sometimes, but all that is required of you is to be positive, never look down on whatever you do. Before you can see the grown plant, it has to be touched by the adequate and accurate amount of water needed, sunlight, air and any other thing you can think of.

No matter how small you're starting, the big picture should never be off your mind; this is what will keep you going during hard and difficult times; times when you feel you're not doing the right thing, times when you think you are not doing enough, times when you feel and wonder if you are doing it the exact way it's meant to be done. The list of doubts and questions are endless it is only left to us to be able to conquer this whenever it comes.

I must tell you it will come whether you expect it or not, it happens, but once you feel you're not doing enough or you're doing too little to reach your success, remember, little drops of water eventually make an ocean. You will soon be celebrated if you don't quit, if you don't give up, if you don't doubt yourself and also your abilities. The big picture, I say again, the big picture, is all you need, make it evident and very foreseeable, sooner than you think you are closer to reaching the maximum height you desire for yourself.

So many times, I doubted myself, even while writing this book I was doubting myself. I kept asking questions like,;who will read what an author who is unknown like me has written? I even asked myself if what I was writing made any sense at all. I wondered if I'll ever become a best-seller. I asked myself if it is possible to be a best-selling author. I asked myself if people will fall in love with what I wrote. Will Oprah Winfrey get to read this book? Will my book be accepted to be sold by amazon? Will the New York Times love my book to the extent of publishing it?

The list goes on.

I called myself to order one day and decided to give it my best shot. I told myself I will be a best-selling author, and esteemed individuals like you will pick up my book to read. They'll be happy reading and learning from me and I will also get good and pleasant comments and also more opportunities will open for me. I am bound to succeed, and I am a success regardless of the fact that I am from Nigeria. As I write this, I feel so much joy. I have been so consumed writing this portion of the book that I didn't realize I missed my dad's call two times. I didn't hear my phone ring. At this juncture, I need to tell you this, YOU WILL BE SUCCESSFUL.

- GET A MENTOR: Mentors are ladders we climb to get a better view of the world, ourselves, and what we are capable of achieving. You will always need a mentor at a particular point in your life. Mentors are positioned to help, guide, and nurture you to the peak of your potential.

There are some stages or situations in life that will seem difficult or impossible to attain or overcome, this is where you need a mentor. A mentor is someone who has gone ahead of you in the aspect, area, or discipline which you may find yourself in at the moment. They also might have gone through that particular stage or phase at one time in their life, business-wise, leadership, family or career. With you having a mentor, you might and would be able to foresee and identify various challenges that may be looming in your areas of engagement. It may also interest you to know that there are things you can discuss with a mentor that you might not be comfortable approaching a colleague, friend or relative with. As earlier mentioned, they generally have more experience, know you well, and can give you the quality advice and feedback you need to succeed.

Now, let's dive in to how to get a mentor. There is an open secret that nobody talks about, but everyone knows. There are shortcuts in life, and I don't mean random life hacks here or there like putting two straws together to make a longer one or removing the middle bun of a Burger. These are nice, but don't really move the needle.

I am talking wisdom to move up the career ladder or how to find a board member to guide your startup and even what to do when you are about to become a husband/father/wife/mother. Perhaps even how to deal with the loss of a loved one or the disintegration of a relationship; romantic or otherwise.

Believe it or not, whatever you are going through—no matter

how seemingly specific—is not unique to you.

I know this is tough to accept because we are all the stars of our own life, and it may feel like our hardships or milestones are somehow categorically common to all mankind, but situationally unique to ourselves. But I'm here to tell you that the specifics don't matter. It's the shared experiences that do. And that's a good thing because it means there is someone out there who has gone through what you have. Be it a positive potential opportunity for which you may be under-prepared, a neutral but unfamiliar stage in life, or a negative and painful event, you can usually find someone who can shine as a guiding light. That person is your mentor. He or she can help you through this wonderful windy journey called life.

The ideal Mentor

In my opinion, there are a few core characteristics of a strong mentor. You can have more than one mentor. No one person knows everything. So you should diversify the guidance you receive from multiple people with valid backgrounds, histories, and experiences. These are the common traits I have come to learn about ideal mentors:

1. They are active listeners. A top mentor will tolerate your complaints, not because they like it, but because in their effort to help you, they will listen so as to unravel your pain points. They are able to help you find the right solution to your peculiar challenges as they listen to you speak. The amazing thing is, mentors are patient enough to allow you finish speaking.

2. They are brutally clear. A strong mentor will not deceive you or waste your time. They will tell you what you need to know. You won't hear a lot of nice qualifying statements, but rather they'll pinpoint the heart of the matter with sharp and concise communication. They treat you like an adult, so they won't sugar coat their words. That means they respect you. If you are messing up, they will tell you without hesitation. But it doesn't mean they are rude or unkind. They're actually objective to a fault.

3. They are hyper specific. A capable mentor often gives you a list of action items. They won't give you a lot of theory. They'll say words like, "Do the following, in the following order…" or "Here is a strategy with a set of must- dos." A good mentor doesn't give you high-level narrative or generalisations. Advice should be actionable, or you might as well read a self-help book. They are likely to be prescriptive, and open about the drawbacks of an action plan, and they leave you to make the final decisions.

4. They are honest about their limitations. A great mentor will tell you when they cannot mentor you on a subject. They will say, "I'm sorry, but I'm out of my depth regarding this particular matter. However, I do know someone who can help you." This is a real mentor. They are not here to dish out garbage advice just to listen to themselves talk. They are humble. They want to help you directly; but when they can't, they will make an effort to connect you with someone who can.

5. They follow up. The best mentors I've had always follow up to see how I'm doing. That means they are really invested in you. They actually care and you should treat that as the most valuable gift, because not only are they giving you time, they are also allocating mindshare to you. Do not take that for granted.

If your mentors follow up, honor them by picking up and responding appropriately. The greatest gift you can give to them is your growth. Be better—take their words and counsel seriously. Actively share updates with them. They will appreciate it.

I'm sure my esteemed readers are eager to know how to find a mentor, and yes, it is important to know how to find a mentor for yourself. You don't need to worry, I'm here for you, and if all is adhered to, you'll be able to get yourself the best mentor.

In the past few paragraphs, we've been talking about some characteristics of mentors, but how then do you find a mentor? That's a question I know might be running through some minds, now this is it.

1- Do not go up to someone with the explicit intent of finding a mentor. It doesn't work that way. Mentoring and being mentored is an organic process that requires you both to invest in a relationship. It doesn't happen overnight. Both parties need to build trust. That means you need to look for mentors without looking for them, which sounds like nonsense at first. But for me at least, each mentor became mentors to me through some form of mutual or shared experience. So, what do you do? You need to focus; pay attention to people who are already near you and have wisdom.

Be humble enough to identify their strengths that complement your weakness. Start there! Then broaden your circle outwardly, over time.

2- Do not be surprised if your mentor is younger than you (different from you). It is a common mistake to believe that age, experience, and wisdom go hand-in-hand. Or any other type of stereotype. Avoid these mentalities and biases. Wisdom can be found in anyone, regardless of age, creed, race, or gender. You need to look for sages, not a white-haired old man, wearing a robe and wielding a staff.

Remember that processing great advice doesn't mean that these mentors have to share the exact same experience as you have.

Rather, it means that regardless of their experience, they have deducted a commonly useful, applicable, and executable pearl of wisdom.

3- Do not be desperate. Sure, to find a good mentor, you must be humble and open minded, but you must also be discerning, meaning you cannot simply accept everyone or anyone as a potential mentor. In other words, don't be falsely humble or falsely open minded. There are tons of bad advisors out there!

Mentorship is a two-way interaction, whether you are mentoring or being mentored. Your mentor is evaluating you, and trying to determine if you are worth their time. You should also be evaluating your mentor. See if their advice, when applied, is making a difference in your life. There are tons of people who want to be mentors (in the form of board membership, career supervisors, etc.) because there is personal and financial gain to get from you as well.

Remember— a mentor is looking for high-potential candidate to have as their mentee too. Successful people help each other grow, and a real mentor is also hoping to learn from you through their mentoring you. It sounds weird, but trust me on this, please.

4- Do not pay someone to be your mentor. Do not quote me

wrong. I am not saying you shouldn't reward your mentor. Yes, it is very important to show appreciation to people who have added value to you one way or another. What I'm saying is, a real mentor isn't going to expect compensation by default, because they genuinely believe that your success is also theirs. They find fulfilment in your growth.

On your end, you should always figure out a way to show gratitude, and that doesn't have to be financial. It can be in form of being helpful when they are in a jam, or connecting them to other helpful people. It can be in the form of smaller gestures too. When all is said and done, your relationship with your mentor shouldn't be reduced to a set of transactions.

5- Do not assume that someone else's mentor can necessarily be yours. As a corollary to numbers 1 and 3 above, you should now understand that finding a mentor is a pretty hard, but achievable task. Most of all, it must take place naturally. It's also about fit. An advisor for one can be a disaster for another, and vice versa. Therefore, you should always determine the mentor-mentee fit based on your personal interaction or experience with a potential mentor.

You will agree with me that our journey so far about mentorship has been an enlightening one, and I am glad I could patiently diffuse all that I needed to pass across. This is a reminder; one way or the other, no matter who we are, there will come a time in our lives, or stage in our businesses where we'll need a mentor.

The value of mentorship is enormous, as a good mentor can be pivotal during major junctures of your life, both personally and professionally. They can steer you clear of disaster, provide prescient views of the future that you can't see, and heal your soul (and even your body, depending on the situation) when you're hurting.

Everyone can find mentors. It's up to you to cherish the relationships you have, cultivate new ones, and never take the people who can help you for granted. Above all, you must recognise that mentors can be everyday people, who have extraordinary advice. They don't have to be superheroes or millionaires or big CEOs.

Before I draw the curtain on mentors, I leave you with this. Remember to also pay it forward. Find your own mentees too.

- PRACTICE, FAIL, START OVER: We can't conclude this chapter without discussing this important aspect- read, practice, fail, start over.

Failure is not a crime, you must be prepared to fail. Failure gives you better insight into the future, it helps you make amends with respect to your past, it builds you up for unforeseen challenges that may further arise during the course of your journey to success. Great men, at a point in their lives, failed. Men of valour have experienced failure as well. You have to learn from all failures and build up your strength, only then will you be catapulted into the future you want and desire for yourself.

So, pick up that pen and write that book, make that phone call, give life to that idea living rent-free in your mind, go all out and make your dream work.

Don't sit and wait to be transported into success; just like I stated earlier, only by practicing will you encounter failures. Failures which will help shine a light on your path. Failing ten thousand and ten times to achieve one outstanding success and breakthrough isn't a crime, remember the place of consistency in this journey to greatness, and of course, discipline, determination, and just as you've read in the previous chapters of this book, your mind must be aligned and directed towards greatness. There's no room for giving up on this journey.

Always endeavour to start over anytime you encounter failures, start over, don't be discouraged. Starting again after failing is easier said than done, but then, you just have to do it. Failure is only an event, it is not the definition of you neither is it attached to any of your names.

Now, let's get serious. While that failure stares at you in the face, you also need to look deep into your failures. Find out what caused your failures, what you did wrong, where it all went wrong, what decisions led to the failures, what steps or experiments did you not do right, what opinion did you follow when on that project, who and what did you consult during the course of practice.

Do everything possible to unravel the answers to these questions. You must exploit the lessons and wisdom that failure has to offer you. Do not forget this. It is only by doing this that you can have the resources to forge ahead on your journey to success.

As I draw the curtain on this chapter, I urge you to own up when you find areas where you made mistakes. Take responsibility for your own errors. I don't mean in a way that sends you down the lane of depression, but in an empowering way. If you can accept the responsibility for those wrong steps you took, then it means you have the power to change course and make the right decisions and take the right steps going forward.

Success Is Free...Only If You Are Ready To Pay The Price

CHAPTER 4

VISION THERAPY

VISION THERAPY

To commence this chapter, I'll take a dive into the meaning of Vision Therapy. It is defined as a behavioural, individualised approach to correcting various eye problems that affect one's ability to receive and process visual information. Here's a quote by Myles Munroe *"People who changed the world have declared independence from other people's expectations."*

Basically, I am saying you have to develop a way to see things, you have to possess a clear vision of what you want and how to get to your destination. You will agree with me that a man without vision cannot go far, and not just any vision, we're talking about a clear vision. Having a vision provides a sense of purpose and direction for the journey to success. Your vision will help you define your long and short-term goals, and guide the decisions you make along the way; your vision is your most important dream or mental picture.

Just so you know the power of vision, if you advance confidently in the direction of your dreams and endeavour to live the life which you have imagined or envisioned, you will meet with the success unexpectedly in common hours. The power of vision can't be disregarded, as without vision, there will definitely be no direction and you keep doing the unnecessary The good news is, once you develop a clear vision and discover yourself, you can rest assured the sky is the starting point.

Here's another lovely quote I love so much and I would like to share with you, it goes, *"If you don't have a vision, you're going to be stuck in what you know, and the only thing you know is what you've already seen"* (Iyanla Vanzant). I tell you; a vision is not just a picture of what could be; it is an appeal to our better selves, a call to become something more.

You really can't do without having a vision; vision of where you want to be, what you want to be, what eventually will happen when you get to where you want to be, and even how to get to that apex point of your dreams. I didn't just pick up my laptop and start writing, NO!! I didn't at all, I had a vision, I saw the big picture, I saw where I wanted to be, and what will happen if that is achieved, I saw how to navigate myself to the apex I saw, and yes, if you've been following me actively, you will notice how I keep mentioning that I'm a freshly baked writer that wants to be known for his tremendous works. I want to make an impact, yes, that is basically the greatest achievement in life. if you would agree with me. Just so you know, I wasn't born with a silver spoon, I really don't care and it doesn't matter how I was born, where I was born, the season I was born, or my race, if I can see it, I am sure going to have it. I will work hard and smart to make my dreams a reality. I'm sure I will, one day, be interviewed by Oprah Winfrey and all other esteemed OAPs and I know some will also be from my readers.

You must understand the power of vision, you must really know what to do when you have one. Your vision, like we've been saying, will be your drive, and , we're not talking spiritual here and I'm not expecting you to have a bad vision, and obviously, I don't think a bad vision will push you towards greatness and success, - there's always a positive vision whenever we talk about our success in life, we can't but see all good, pleasant and positive visions, I stand to be corrected if peradventure there are also bad visions to success- feel free to hit me up, my contact details are right behind the book. You must have a clear vision, not a blurry one, if you find it blurry, commence, take a step! An action is all you need to get your vision clearer. In this course will you discover your true, clear vision, you can't get a clear(er) vision by just staying put with the blurry vision you have, and yes, I'm talking from experience.

Sometimes, you don't really have it all figured out, yes, you have a vision, but then, you've got some questions concerning some aspects of your visions (visions not one), you are an unlimited being, you are open to various and thousands of visions, you have to keep seeing and seeing, don't be tired of seeing or having a vision.

For every vision you have, make sure you pick up your pen and write them down. Don't give up on your dreams, don't be tired of seeing. You might be saying to yourself, "Is this possible?" "Can this be?" I'm telling you again, friend, if you don't have it all figured out, it's not a problem. Don't be too hard on yourself. Hold on to the vision you have received.

A quick one here, do you know a vision can lead to another? Here's another one, esteemed readers, just as our faces are different so are our visions, we all are unique and distinct, we've got various drives, weaknesses and strengths. I know mine, and I have come to understand this about myself; whenever I want to achieve the best of all, be it my projects or anything I'm personally engaged in as a path to being successful, I have to do them either in the middle of the night or in the early hours of the morning. You also have your own, work with what's best for you, you don't need to force yourself, take your time, but don't take too much of time. You need to make hay while the sun shines.

Your vision is different from mine, so go ahead and ride all the way to your success.

Here is another tip for you, always speak well of yourself and consistently visualise your life working out as you want it. This is very important as it is a force that also drives you to your destination, and it, sometimes, is much faster than you think.

Speak to life that great vision of yours, don't stop saying it, even if it seems it's not happening as soon as you had expected, continue with this and someday, you'll sit back and remember all, then you know what happens after? You develop a big smile, oh! Did I really smile while writing that? Okay! It's fine! I smiled, and you know what that smile does to you? It releases more positivity needed for you to carry on to the next phase of your success journey, because you really don't need an eye to see, you need vision.

"Vision without action is merely a dream. Action without vision just

passes the time. Vision with action can change the world" (Joel A. Barker). I won't feel good if I actually skip this part; you need to know the characteristics of a vision, here are a few;

- Clarity
- Abstract and challenging
- Future focused
- Sets a desirable goal

All you need do is to endeavour your vision has got these characteristics, and you are on the right path. Your journey to being successful is closer than you could think! Don't forget, the road to success won't always be smooth and remember, *"When the going gets tough, the tough gets going"*. This has been a quote I have memorised since I was young and it has always been my drive even when I hadn't discovered myself.

Take that step of faith, take that action, and trust me, you will make it!!

CHAPTER 

CHARACTER THERAPY

"There is no adversity that cannot be overcome by good character"

- Michael S. Josephson.

What a person says and does in ordinary moments when no one is looking reveals more about their character than grand actions taken while in the spotlight. Our true character is revealed by normal, consistent, everyday attitudes and behaviours, not by self-conscious words or deeds or rare acts of moral courage. This is to make known to you that character is determined by how we live our lives, how we deal with life's unearned fortunes and misfortunes, and how we make choices that determine how those fortunes and misfortunes work to make us what we become.

The character therapy has a very important role to play on your way to success, and in fact, without this, the probability of being successful is limited; this is the reason why this key shouldn't be taken for granted. Sometimes, it is your character that defines who you really are; just as I have rightly explained above, it is a must to have and develop a good character. It's never too late to start. Okay, let me guess, you'll hear some say, "This is what and who I am and I can't change it." I put it to you that you can change. You can make that change now because it can be a hindrance on the path to your success. Just as you know, there is no way you want to thread the path of success that you won't, one way or another need people. I am so sure that 99.9% of successful people at one point or the other had to relate with certain people. The people you meet on your path to journey are the connecting rods to your success. In other words, they are your connections.

The value of your good character in relating with people can't be overemphasised, it is a constant hurdle that must be crossed.

I would like to share with you one of my posts on LinkedIn, I wrote:

"Character is a simple nine letter word that is often disregarded, misused, and also greatly used to the fullest by man." I want you to know that character can't be put under cover in anything that we do, no matter our profession, position, race, or ethnicity. It is so important, as it is a determinant for our future, or let me say destiny;

many might argue. If I get a good job, and work hard, I'll be successful, I'll achieve my goals. We tend to forget the propelling factor aside all mentioned above. Most people even think they can pray their way to achieve success and get away with virtually anything. There's no amount of spiritual penance that can substitute character! We must learn to treat people with courtesy and respect. We can easily judge the character of a man by the way he treats people who can do nothing for him, people who he thinks can't help or hurt him. So, I say to you, character is destiny, since character can change, so can destiny; so, no matter who you are and where you are from, you can become great and fulfil destiny."

A good character helps you develop a winning personality. In other words, a good character is the magnetic personality which attracts other people. I must tell you that once you have a good character, you are always available to these benefits, such as, achieving peace of mind, strengthened trust, it helps you build a solid reputation, anxiety reduction, increase in leadership effectiveness, confidence and you becoming a positive role model

Let me show you some traits of exceptional character that lead to success and happiness:

- Honesty: At the core of any person with a good character is honesty. You tend to do what is right, and never cheat or lie to get ahead of the curve. Honesty is what separates the activator from procrastinator, the dreamer from the doer, and the successful from the non-successful. When it comes to character, we are not what we think, we are not what we say, we are what we do.

- Survival: Character is largely developed from suffering the trials and errors of life. Survivors stay through to the end. People with this trait don't quit,. People of exceptional character do not quit when times get tough, nor treat others terribly when things don't go their way.

People of exceptional character have faith and tough-mindedness to stay in the grind and get things accomplished, regardless of the odds. There is a lot to be said about staying power. The more others quit under the same stressors, the more opportunity and grit the person of good character has to make sure to secure what they set out to achieve.

- Leadership: When you possess good character, leadership is the natural side effect. The truth is, people want to follow those who have suffered, those who possess self-awareness, patience and the ability to rise. No matter their title in the business world, people of exceptional character draw a followership with word of mouth, supporting and promoting their reputation as someone others should invest in learning from and working with. When a person's character is authentic, they have a quiet resolve about them that others feel compelled to trust, emulate and follow.

-Elegance: Still talking about character, you must know that self-control is one of the most powerful traits of people who possess exceptional character. They have a calm demeanour and this demonstrated in their ability to be patient and to listen to others. It takes a certain amount of self-control to listen rather than talk. It is this elegant nature of those with good character that not only makes them a bit mysterious, but also so interesting to others. People of good character recognise that gentleness is their greatest strength. They are above the pettiness of right and wrong when in conflict or facing a challenge. They are more interested in finding the path to the solution that involves inclusion and innovation.

-Hard Work: Show me anyone who wants to succeed without working hard and smart and I'll tell you the person is either looking for a short cut to success, which at the end is destructive, or is just wasting their time. In order to build up good character, the place of hard work can't be neglected. Good character and hard work go hand in hand. None of us was born with good character; good character is developed over time and through the virtues of hard work and commitment. We cannot develop our character without having to work hard and suffer through times of conflict and challenge. The reason hard work develops character is because it is the only thing that can outdo and outlast both genius and talent.

Good character is worth going hard for. In fact, I will tell you that how high you rise on your journey to success is determined by your good character; you can't shove that aside. On your path or journey to success, you will come across different types of people, people from different backgrounds, races, cultures, tribes, and numerous beliefs and perspectives about life, so the way you co-exist with all you come across is determined by your character.

To be frank with you, often times, you will come across people you wish and hope you didn't come across; people who have a different belief from the general human belief, but truth be told, you have to pass through them on your journey to success. I'm sure most of us have had an encounter with some on our way to success, either they're in charge of signing your contract or they make the final decision on your product or services, or all they will do is just cross-check your proposal, product, or idea. The truth be told, in the place where you've got a good exceptional character, you will agree with me that such people can be penetrated without you stressing at all. Do not forget this, and I don't mind if it's only this one thing you will remember in this part of the book, "Your character defines who you truly are", it is the mirror that portrays to the world who you are. Even without you opening your mouth and telling people about your personality, they tend to identify you by your character. Having a good character can earn you favour from men who you think are difficult to gain access to.

With a good character, people will pick interest in you and you will agree with me that that's basically the beginning of success.

Good character is important for success in your life, because it determines how well you can achieve your goals, whether others want to deal with you, and how well you fit in your groups.

When you work hard and are determined to achieve your goals, you can become more successful and confident in what you do. Now, I know some reading will say to themselves,

"What then can I do to develop a good and exceptional character?"

It's simple, time tests; character erodes or grows. Our character is developed through time. More accurately, our character is developed through our experiences and what we choose to learn and do from them, so the question is what do you choose from the experiences of life? That's basically how your character is developed, you have the right to choose what you want to adopt, learn from, it's a personal work that needs to be carried out wholeheartedly.

In general, people are considered to have good character when they possess the following traits like, honesty, courage, humility, loyalty, fortitude, integrity, and other important virtues that promote good behaviour. These traits define who they are as people—and highly influence the choices they make in their lives.

Before I drop the ink on character as a key, here's a little summary. Character is important for success as it's what makes us authentic. It makes us who we are. Being self-aware about character is what will make you stand out in a good way.

In the meantime, as an individual, don't blame others (those above, on same level with, or below you professionally) for a lack of ethics and character, but commit to being the character that you would want to be led by.

Don't just argue what you believe is good but practice it too.

Don't forget a good character builds the trust needed for success.

CHAPTER 6

ACTION THERAPY

ACTION THERAPY

"The only impossible journey is the one you never begin."

- Tony Robbins.

Action, they say, speaks louder than words, and I believe and accept this fact. Working only with your words and imagination is not enough to guarantee your success. Action is required.

In this chapter of the book, we will carefully analyse the "Action Therapy" which is essential in the journey to success. You might have heard the saying, *"little droplets of water make an ocean,"* put differently, it means doing something, no matter how little, will yield great rewards in the end. This is why you can't just have all the ideas right in your head and fail to birth them. The reality is, you will be on the same spot you are right now in 5 year's time if you do not take intentional actions from now. Ideas and innovations can't manifest themselves without action. They got into your head somehow, and in there, they are waiting for manifestation and to be brought to limelight. That is where your riches and success lie.

You can't be great or do exploits by just folding your arms and watching things happen; you can't accomplish anything that way.

Here is the thing, friends, the very moment you take that bold step concerning your ideas and innovations, you are 20% into the completion of your journey to success, yes, 20% out of a 100% so you know the next bold step earns you another 20%, so why the delay? I am going to say this here: **What you want and desire is on the other side of your fears.**

You really need to sit, reflect and highlight the possible obstacles preventing you from taking that bold step.

I am proud to say this, over here, where I come from, amongst all odds, great minds in the country have since continued to take the bold step towards making their dreams and aspirations come true. This development has since increased overtime. I am proud to say I'm amongst that great number of people taking action and doing great things and I hope to impact more lives.

Few would actually say writing a book isn't a hard thing to do. It's actually tough. This particular book took me months to complete and publish, looking at all I have to put together in writing, I had to be determined to take this action. I must tell you the odds were much, and without self-determination, nothing would have been achieved, with the present economic crises, the pandemic and all other odds.

Now, let me show you something here, the idea of writing a book wasn't the first idea I conceived. I had other ideas, but they could not be achieved without a lot of funds. I was bent on getting something done and not delay any longer. I saw there was no fast way to get these great ideas accomplished but of course, I knew there was just one thing to do which won't cost me a huge sum of funds. So I said to myself, "Since I have the flare for writing, why don't I harness my writing skill to produce a book?"

If I could come out at the end of the day with this great book, funds will come in which can be used for other purposes. Do not forget I was actually taking action, and by doing this, I made progress. I'm moving, gaining traction, pushing my work to the limelight, my voice, and thoughts are being heard around the world through writing. You will agree with me that even places I can't get to at the moment, just an E-copy of my book could fly to such countries and change lives.

Do you really know how much I have been able to accomplish just by thinking smart and taking just one action towards great success? You might be wondering why I used the words "Great success" and not just "Success." There is a difference and the difference is in the word "GREAT." I don't just want to have any sort or form of success.

It is good to have huge, viable ideas, but then, what do you do when you are short of funds and all efforts to find investors yield no tangible result? Do you give up? Or do you keep pushing till something comes up? Remember while doing that, a lot of time and energy is being consumed, but of course, if you can see it, you can have it. If it is worth it, why not continue to go after it? You must keep making progress. Stagnation is not acceptable! If you notice you are not moving, change your course, look into other directions, there are numerous things that can be done.

Until the action therapy is understood and practised, there is always a limit to what we can accomplish. There are points in life when it will seem difficult to take a bold step, and you wonder if whatever you do will actually make a meaning or impact. This, I tell you, is the point when you shouldn't look at the odds but go ahead and take that action, take that bold step.

Sometimes, you see your ideas as huge and maybe unreasonable or unrealistic or impossible, but if you look deep you will see the light at the end of the tunnel if you press on with this great idea. If you're wondering where to start from, I am asking you to start right where you are; just begin from where you are and with what you have, you will be amazed at the incredible progress you will make on your journey.

The path to success requires action.

You will agree with me, that all the keys listed in this great book are interwoven and you need them all at one point or the other. At some point, you might need just one key, and at another moment, you might need the combination of two keys to unlock your journey to success.

An idea not coupled with action will never get any bigger than the brain cell it occupies. You need to know this; you really don't need to over-think what your end results will be, let your performance do the talking. People may doubt what you say, but they will believe what you do.

Please note this, you must always be contented to act and leave the talking to others, and of course you must know this, "God provides the winds, but man must raise the sails." God has His own part, and you also have your part to play. Most people just blindly put all in God's hands and refuse to do anything on their part. They say these worrisome words, "If God does not make this work, who am I to do anything or take any step?" You really don't know how pissed I get when I hear these words. The words don't work every time. We all have a part to play- do your part, take that action and stop throwing words around! If you really want to know who you are, you need not ask, all you need do is act. Action will dictate and define who you truly are.

My esteemed readers, it is a must you know inaction breeds doubts and fear. Action breeds confidence and courage. If you want to conquer fear, do not sit at home and think about it. Go out and get busy. Go out! Leave your comfort zone, you can't have everything coming to meet you where you're sitting or lying down thinking. Your thoughts (without action) won't change anything.

This book in your hands wouldn't have become a reality if I didn't take action, mobilize the necessary resources and follow through to the very end. Along the way I got tired, weary and even almost got discouraged. But I persisted. The finish line kept me going all through. There is a certain standard of living I want for myself, there are numerous ideas that need to be birthed; these, I took as my drive. They were the ones pushing me through this journey of great success and I have grown to know that action is the antidote to despair. I also know outstanding people have one thing in common – an absolute sense of mission, meaning if you really desire and want to be outstanding, if you have admired great outstanding individuals and sometimes you want to be more like them and do great things than they have done, you have to possess an absolute sense of mission. A mission driven with vision will bring success.

There is, of course, one proof of ability and that is action. There will always be someone who can't see your worth, don't let it be you! Excuses are thieves of time!!! Always have a goal, accept responsibility and take action.

Before I end this chapter, I will leave you with this quote *"A man is the sum of his actions, of what he has done, of what he can do. Nothing else"*- Mahatma Gandhi.

94

CHAPTER 7

HUMILITY

HUMILITY

"Real genius is nothing else but the supernatural virtue of humility in the domain of thought."

Simone Weil.

This last chapter focuses on the most important ingredient needed to reach the peak of our potential and to achieve great success. Without this important key, it will be difficult to maintain one's track record of success. Humility is a virtue which must be cultivated in our lives. Of course, we can't talk about humility without mentioning its opposite, pride.

Here is a wise saying from a famous Chinese philosopher and writer, *"I have three precious things which I hold fast and prize. The first is gentleness; the second is frugality; the third is humility, which keeps me from putting myself before others. Be gentle and you can be bold; be frugal and you can be liberal; avoid putting yourself before others and you can become a leader among men"* (Lao Tzu).

Humility is said to be the quality of being humble, it propels an individual to a high level of greatness. Humility, most times, brings all you have ever desire with ease, you may want to ask why I said that, here's why; people who are not full of themselves earn themselves honor and respect from people around them. Humility is an attribute of great leaders. Humility doesn't reduce you at all, rather it adds to you- do not forget this- humility is the fuel of light, and light is the fuel for distinction.

It is essential to note that humility makes your journey smooth and your ascent to greatness easy. It gives you the grace needed, draws potential life-changing individuals to you without you having to go scouting for them. This virtue should and must be a part of us, and it must be practiced each and every day of our lives.

Pride often irritates other people. Individuals who feel bigger and better than others are not in any way attractive. People may be forced to be with them only because of what they have to offer, asides that, it would be difficult to truly build meaningful relationships with them. And when such individuals fall, it is often very fatal because no one will be willing to stick out their necks for them. Pride, indeed, goes before a fall.

My esteemed reader, humility is the doorway of insight, light and revelation. You really have to be humble to get insights for your journey.

Life is in phases. You do not know everything there is to know about your journey now. This is why humility is required to access all (new relationships, opportunities, etc) that is still ahead of you. If you need to read this over and over again, please do so because here lies greatness and many tend to underestimate the power of humility. To be successful, you need insight and foresight. I mentioned earlier that humility brings you into contact with valuable people. Put simply, humility attracts the right people to you.

At every point on your journey, these people come to you with ideas and plans about how to make your next big hit. You might also be lucky to have them share with you what directions and paths they've since been taking on this journey to success.

You need foresight to see further and you need insight to see things differently.

Humility is a key to leadership; it keeps you ahead of the pack. Always remain humble at all times, even if you have achieved so much and have gotten to the peak of your career, remember there are many who have been in the same exact point and stage of life you are presently. I must say this, it baffles me anytime I see an individual who hasn't achieved anything meaningful, yet full of pride. We also must not forget those who have just begun their journey becoming proud with their little achievements. Irrespective of who you know, where you've been and the little accolades you've received, always remain conscious of the bigger things that are ahead of you.

Pride should not be an option for you. The earlier you wake up to realise this, the better for you.

I've heard a number of people deny that they are proud. On the surface, it may be true, but then, it takes someone else to really help you know exactly if you are proud or not. Usually as a defense, such people might say, "I know I'm not proud." I have been in this situation before. A number of people have also told me that I am proud. Rather than defend myself, I often choose to evaluate myself to see if their assertions about me are true or false.

After completing your personal check up, and reminiscing on all that transpired, you need to tell yourself the truth, if you can't see or can't see yourself being proud, good! Work on yourself and make humility a lifestyle.

Let me see if I can read your minds, you're about to ask me how one can see if he or she is proud, isn't it? I must say that's a very good question, and I'm here to explain that to you.

How do you know you are proud or struggling with pride?

1- When you think you are humble.

One of the signs that you are proud is if you refuse to admit that you struggle with pride. Saying to people that you are humble doesn't actually mean you are. You need to stop telling yourself-or others-that you are humble. If that is true, then let others acknowledge it.

2- You find it difficult to (or do not) accept constructive criticisms.

Proud people have a hard time accepting failure. For this reason, they refuse to be corrected. They are always offended whenever their behaviour is scrutinised. The easiest way to get this is for you to be thankful when others correct you because it will help you improve. Remember, you are not perfect.

3- You always want to be the centre of attention

This is self-explanatory. You don't become respected by being the loudest voice in the room. Quit trying to be the center of every conversation you get into. This is yet another thorn you must remove from your life. Do not think you are more important than anyone else. We are all valuable and as such, build a habit of listening to others and valuing their opinion.

You probably would have come across such individuals at one point or another on your journey through life, and if you are such an individual, you need to change.

4- You are vain about your physical appearance

Being obsessed about making yourself attractive is another hint of pride creeping into you. In connection with no. 3, vanity makes you flaunt your beauty with the hope that you will be admired my everyone. Please do not get this wrong. It is okay to take good care of yourself, but evaluate your motives. If it's to draw attention to yourself, then maybe it's time to re-orientate yourself about what real beauty is.

5- You do not like associating with the "ordinary" or unpopular

This, also, has since been a trait of pride, and you would agree with me that we have close pals or relatives who behave exactly like the above. Most times when you walk up to them, the reception you get from them is, most times, disheartening. If you really think you only deserve professionals and "first-class" citizens as friends and you avoid hanging out with "low-level" people, then you are clearly prideful.

To get rid of this attitude, treat people equally. Make friends, not according to social status, but the sincerity of individuals towards you. Associating with people who do not have any title attached to their names will not make you cheap.

6- You are fond of name-dropping

This is an aspect I find very disturbing and confusing at the same time and I often ask myself, "Does it really matter?"

I really can't comprehend why it must be a name-dropping session at any slightest opportunity for some people. I have been in contact with many of such individuals and I wonder how they find satisfaction in only dropping big names. If you have the habit of talking about your connections with influential, rich, or powerful personalities, then it means you only want to look successful in the eyes of those you speak with.

The people you talk with are probably annoyed listening to you go on and on about your "connections". Be more interested in being successful than looking successful.

7- You are not teachable

Not listening to someone who is trying to teach you something is another sign of pride. It is either you think you know things already or you think you know more than the person. It could also mean you consider him/her inferior to you. Having a teachable heart is one of the traits of humility, you can't be humble and refuse or ignore teaching and correction. A humble person always want to learn.

8- *You don't listen to other people's advice*

Proud people are also stubborn. They think they know it all, they believe they know everything already so they disregard the counsel of others. You are one of them if you brush off advice, whether from your parents, friends, spouse. Begin the process to personal transformation by listening to your parents, teachers, mentors and other important individuals around you. While it is important to receive advice and counsel from people, where you receive the counsel from also matters. Discern the people in your life and know who to give your "ear-time" to.

9- *You do not like to be surpassed by anyone*

Considering others as threat to your position, fame, and success is a function of pride. Your achievement could have gotten into you already making you think you should always be number 1.

Thus, when you meet people who have the potential to surpass your accomplishments, you consider them as rivals and, perhaps, enemies. The sky is wide enough for many birds to fly around without collision. Competition is only healthy if you compete with your past self. Instead of focusing on being ahead of others, why not focus on improving yourself?

10- You think you are too important to do mundane things

This is everywhere-in families, among siblings, at every work station or offices, organisations, to mention a few. If you think your position is so high that you cannot pick up trash, help clean up, or serve others, then that is definitely pride. If you are too big to serve, then you are too small to lead. Being humble has a lot to do with service. I hope you can see how this is interwoven, that is exactly how life is, this is exactly what life is teaching us. On our journey or quest for success, we should be ready to serve.

This does not necessarily mean becoming a slave and a doormat for everyone to thread on. Great people are not afraid to serve those who are not as privileged as they are.

Just before I drop my pen, I would like to mention a few things. Evaluate your heart because there are many other things that could give you a hint that pride is attacking you. The bottom line here is your motivation.

If you do things for selfish purposes, then you are definitely prideful. In order to prevent pride from overcoming you, it is necessary that you check your motives daily. It is important that you keep your feet on the ground no matter how high you have reached already.

Always remember this quote *"The only true wisdom is in knowing you know nothing."*

Now I'm sure you are convinced that success is free only if you pay the price.

ABOUT THE AUTHOR

Adeeko Olalekan is an Entrepreneur, Research Analyst, Public Speaker, Web Developer, and Fintech Enthusiast.

He is one of the founders of TRANSFORM HER AFRICA; an organization that educates about gender equality for the girl child and women. They provide support for the gender across Africa and they look to expand their coast outside the shores of the continent.

He also has a Podcast by the name gidiTalk which is available on Spotify, Anchor, Google Podcasts, and other Podcast platforms.